Emiliano Zapata

A Proud Heritage The Hispanic Library

Emiliano Zapata

*Revolutionary and
Champion of Poor Farmers*

R. Conrad Stein

Published in the United States of America by The Child's World®
PO Box 326 • Chanhassen, MN 55317-0326 • 800-599-READ • www.childsworld.com

Acknowledgments
    The Childs World®: Mary Berendes, Publishing Director
    Editorial Directions, Inc.: E. Russell Primm, Editorial Director; Pam Rosenberg, Project Editor;
    Melissa McDaniel, Line Editor; Katie Marsico, Assistant Editor; Matt Messbarger, Editorial
    Assistant; Susan Hindman, Copyeditor; Susan Ashley and Sarah E. De Capua, Proofreaders;
    Chris Simms and Olivia Nellums, Fact Checkers; Timothy Griffin/IndexServ, Indexer; Cian
    Loughlin O'Day and Dawn Friedman, Photo Researchers; Linda S. Koutris, Photo Selector
    Creative Spark: Mary Francis and Rob Court, Design and Page Production
    Cartography by XNR Productions, Inc.

Photos
    Cover: Detail from *Emiliano Zapata* by Diego Rivera on the Palace of Cortés in
    Cuernavaca, Mexico
    Cover photograph: Archivo Iconografico, S.A./Corbis
    Interior photographs: The Art Archive/Antochiw Collection, Mexico/ Mireille Vautier: 15;
    Bettmann/Corbis: 8, 12, 18, 19, 21, 25, 26, 31; Corbis: 7, 9 (Robert Holmes), 11 (Hulton-
    Deutsch Collection), 14 (ML Sinibaldi), 28 (Underwood & Underwood), 29 (Jeremy
    Horner); Getty Images: 20 (Stephen Dunn), 23 (Time Life Pictures); Getty Images/
    Hulton|Archive: 10, 27, 32; Getty Images/Liaison: 35-top (Stephen Ferry), 35-bottom
    (Wesley Bocxe); Getty Images/ Roger Viollet: 22, 30, 33; Magnum Pictures/Paul Fusco: 34.

Library of Congress Cataloging-in-Publication Data
    Cataloging-in-Publication data for this title has been applied for and is available from the
    United States Library of Congress.

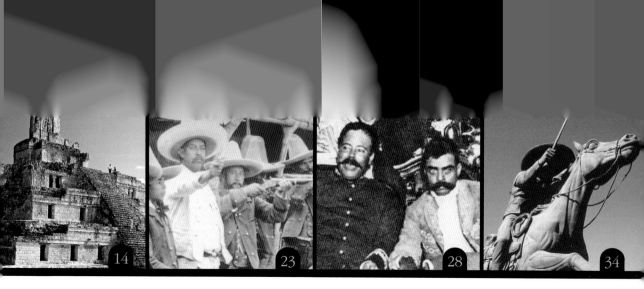

A Zapata Legend

Like many young boys, Emiliano Zapata believed his father was the strongest man in the world. The Zapata family lived in a town of about 400 people in southern Mexico. Most of the townspeople were farmers. Emiliano's father, Gabriel Zapata, was a respected community leader.

One day, when Emiliano was nine years old, a local landowner rode into the village on a tall horse. The owner approached five or six small houses on the outskirts of town. He ordered the people in the houses to come outside. Then he announced that their houses were illegal structures on his land. All families must move at once because he intended to **demolish** the houses and create grazing land for his horses.

The people forced out of their homes appealed to Gabriel Zapata for help. They said they had paid for the

Horsemen ride on farmland in Mexico. Emiliano Zapata grew up in a small farming town in southern Mexico.

land. Some even had papers to prove the land was theirs. But Gabriel Zapata, the most honored man in the village, turned and walked away from his now homeless neighbors.

Later, Emiliano saw his father kneeling in a village orchard. He was weeping. His friends had come to him for help, but he was unable to give them any aid at all. "Why didn't you fight the landowner?" asked young Emiliano. "I can't," said his father. "The owner is too strong."

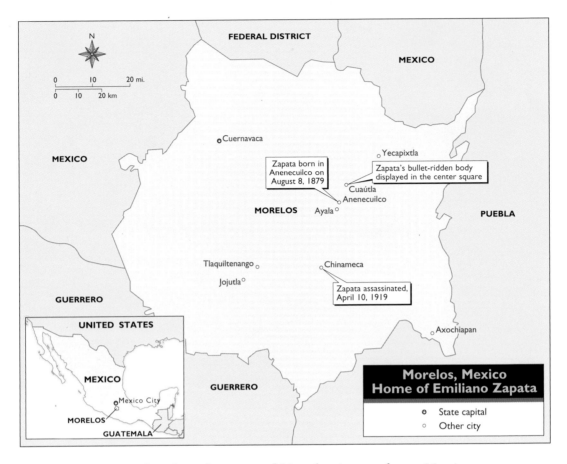

Emiliano Zapata lived in the state of Morelos in southern Mexico.

This story about Emiliano Zapata and his father has been told again and again. No one knows if the story is true or if it is a **legend.** Emiliano Zapata is a celebrated hero of Mexico, and legends are often told about heroes. But whether or not it is true, the story does illustrate how Zapata became devoted to the poor farmers of southern Mexico. Through legal trickery, many farmers lost their land to rich and powerful plantation owners. Zapata led impoverished farmers during the Mexican

Revolution (1910–1920)—an intense time of bloody warfare. Land ownership was a key reason for the fighting. Zapata's battle cry was simple and clear— LAND AND LIBERTY!

Troubled Mexico

Emiliano Zapata was born August 8, 1879 (some records say he was born in 1880), in the village of Anenecuilco. Located south of Mexico City in the state of Morelos, Anenecuilco is an ancient settlement. It dates back to when the Aztec Indians ruled this part of Mexico.

Zapata and his neighbors had Indian bloodlines. Most of them were poor. Wealth in those days was based on land. In Zapata's region, huge sugar plantations stood next to tiny cornfields worked by peasant farmers. The cornfields seemed like checkerboard squares when compared to the plantation land that spread over thousands of acres.

Many wealthy landowners in Mexico lived on large haciendas—ranches or plantations—in homes with beautiful courtyards such as this.

In Zapata's village, many of his neighbors lived in simple homes made of mud and sticks.

Ownership of land had long been a bitter issue in Mexico. Poor farmers owned small plots of land or worked on collective farms called *ejidos* (eh-HEE-dos). Under the ejido system, all members of a village owned shares in a common farm. They worked together in the fields, and divided the food and the profits at harvesttime. Ejido farming was a tradition dating back hundreds of years in Mexico. In contrast to the small farm or the ejido was the fabulously rich farm called a hacienda (ah-see-EN-da). The hacienda might be a cattle ranch or sugar or coffee plantation.

Haciendas occupied rich, well-watered land and often employed more than 100 field hands.

Emiliano Zapata lived in comfortable circumstances compared to his neighbors. His family owned a solid house made of adobe brick. Most other villagers lived in huts fashioned out of mud and sticks. The Zapatas had a small farm of their own and several head of cattle. Emiliano attended a church school long enough to learn basic reading and writing. Many of his neighbors could not even sign their own names.

A handsome man, Emiliano Zapata was sought after by the young women of his village. But he did not marry until age 32, which made him an old bachelor by village standards. He was friendly, but talked very little. When angered, his eyes seemed to cast a glow as if they were on fire.

From an early age, Zapata loved horses. His father sold and

Emiliano Zapata was a handsome young man who was an expert horseman.

Porfirio Díaz served as president of Mexico from 1877 to 1880 and again from 1884 to 1911. He resigned in 1911 and left the country. He died in Paris, France, in 1915.

trained them. Emiliano bred horses, bought and sold them, and **groomed** them until their coats gleamed. Zapata possessed the grace of an athlete, which allowed him to become a marvelous horseback rider. He often put on trick riding displays at rodeos. Spectators hailed him as the best horseman in southern Mexico.

Zapata's relative comfort could not shield him from the **turmoil** boiling up in his country. An ex-army general named Porfirio Díaz served as president of Mexico. President Díaz wanted to make Mexico a modern country, similar to the United States, its neighbor to the to north. However, the president ruled as an iron-fisted **dictator,** and his closest allies included the rich landowners.

President Díaz believed large haciendas produced crops more efficiently than did small farms or ejidos.

12

So Díaz favored laws that allowed hacienda owners to take over land owned by peasant farmers. The results were a disaster for the peasants. In 1895, 20 percent of the people in Mexico reported that they owned land or shares in an ejido. By 1910, only 2 percent claimed to be landowners. Meanwhile, the property holdings of the rich became enormous.

Scores of farmers who had lost land to the haciendas lived in Anenecuilco. When the farmers took their cases to court, the judges always sided with the rich people. In 1909, villagers who had lost ejido land asked Emiliano Zapata to take their case to the governor of Morelos. Zapata told the governor that the farmers faced starvation because they had no land on which to plant their corn. The governor dismissed Zapata with the words, "If the people of Anenecuilco want to grow corn, let them grow it in a flowerpot."

Zapata was drafted into the military. When he returned, he again tried to use legal means to help the poor farmers. But it became clear that it wasn't going to work. Back in Anenecuilco, Zapata made a grave announcement to the farmers. He said they could not trust their government to return the land stolen by hacienda owners. Instead, they must get horses and guns and retake the land by force.

Hundreds of years ago, Native American nations thrived in Mexico. The Maya civilization spread over southern Mexico and much of Guatemala. Farther north, the Aztecs built great pyramids and temples in present-day Mexico City and the surrounding regions.

In 1519, a Spanish adventurer named Hernando Cortés led an army into the Aztec capital at Mexico City. At first, the Aztecs believed Cortés was a god, but war soon broke out between the Aztecs and the Spaniards. After dozens of terrible battles, Cortés conquered the Aztecs and ushered in Spanish rule.

For almost 300 years, the flag of Spain flew above Mexican soil. The Spaniards brought their language and the Catholic religion to Mexico. Many churches and villages were built. Mexicans, however, yearned for freedom. In 1810, Mexican patriots rallied behind a village priest named Miguel Hidalgo y Costilla (below) and launched an independence movement. By the end of 1821, Mexico had won independence from Spain.

This victory did not bring peace, however. In a disastrous war with the United States (1846–1848), Mexico lost its northern territories. These territories included the present-day U.S. states of Texas and California. A series of revolutions and civil wars also gripped the land. President Porfirio Díaz, who took charge in 1876, ended the warfare. But over time, the president's policies triggered the Mexican Revolution of 1910–1920.

Chapter Two

Revolution!

Rage over government policies was not confined to the peasant farmers in southern Mexico. In the north, factory workers and railroad workers toiled for wages that paid barely enough to feed a family. Police jailed or beat up labor leaders who tried to organize unions. Labor became so cheap that it cost a boss more per day to rent a mule than it did to hire a man.

A new and passionate cry—Revolution!—swept Mexico. After years of suffering terrible poverty, the lower classes became a willing army. In the north, impoverished farmers and workers rallied behind Pancho Villa. A one-time cattle rustler, Villa led bands of horsemen who robbed trains and raided cattle ranches to finance revolutionary operations. In the south, farmers answered the call of their leader— Emiliano Zapata.

Revolutionaries take over a train in Veracruz, Mexico. To pay for the revolution, the revolutionaries robbed trains and raided cattle ranches.

The Zapata movement concentrated on retaking land stolen by rich hacienda owners. Zapata's followers knocked down the stone walls of haciendas and moved onto land which had been previously taken from them by courts. They farmed the land while wearing rifles slung over their shoulders. When police tried to force them off the land, gun battles broke out. As the hacienda warfare heated up, the governor of Morelos fled his state. "These are difficult times," the governor said. "The peasant is now the master."

To take over one heavily guarded hacienda, Zapata used a tactic that a modern-day tank commander would admire. In the middle of the night, Zapata's men overpowered the crew of a stopped train. The train operated on a single track, which led to a large hacienda. Zapata ordered his men to board the train's boxcars and coal cars. He then sent the train crashing into the hacienda gate. The surprised hacienda guards quickly surrendered.

In May 1911, President Porfirio Díaz quietly left his office in Mexico City. He had ruled the country for more than 30 years. Now, with uprisings raging in the north and the south, he boarded a ship and sailed to France. The 81-year-old Díaz never returned to Mexico. An honest election was held in October 1911. Francisco Madero was elected president. Madero was a wealthy landowner, but he was known to feed the children of peasant farmers at his own table. Mexicans hoped that the new president would ease the sufferings of the nation's poor.

President Madero met with Zapata. Madero said that farmers in the south should regain the land they lost to the haciendas. But, Madero claimed, the hacienda owners ought to be paid for the disputed land. Zapata thought this idea was ridiculous. After all, the land was originally **confiscated** from the peasant farmers, and no one even suggested paying them. Zapata returned to the south and ordered his farmers to work their land and fight anyone who tried to take it away.

Francisco Madero (shown here shortly before he became president) was a wealthy landowner who sometimes fed the children of poor peasants at his own dinner table.

Mexicans are proud of their very stirring national anthem. It is played before sporting events and during ceremonies on national holidays. The song was declared the country's national anthem in 1854. This was just six years after Mexico lost a war with the United States. Perhaps because of that defeat, the words to the song are **militaristic:**

Mexicanos, al grito de guerra
El acero aprestad y el bridón
Y retiemble en sus centros la tierra
Al sonoro rugir del cañón

Mexicans, at the cry of battle
Prepare your swords and bridle
And let the earth tremble at its center
At the roar of the cannon

Madero proved to be more of a dreamer than a doer. The president angered the rich by claiming to favor land reform, and at the same time he frustrated the poor by failing to act. Ambitious military men sought to overthrow Madero. In 1913, General Victoriano Huerta kidnapped Madero and later ordered him shot. With

People mourn at the grave of President Francisco Madero. The Mexican Revolution entered its most violent, bloodiest stage after his murder.

Emiliano Zapata, ready for battle at the beginning of the Mexican Revolution.

Madero's death, the Mexican Revolution of 1910–1920 entered its bloodiest stage.

The Plan of Ayala

On November 27, 1911, a band composed of drummers and horn players assembled in the tiny Morelos town of Ayala. The musicians were peasant farmers who wore white cotton outfits. Standing at attention, they played the Mexican national anthem. At the conclusion of the anthem, Emiliano Zapata stepped out of a country hut. He wore the flag of Mexico wrapped around him like a cloak.

As several hundred people watched in awe, Zapata read a document that contained his vision of Mexico's future. The document was called the Plan of Ayala. Land reform was the plan's focal point. Zapata called for legal deeds to be given at once to all farmers who now worked land they had taken from the haciendas.

He also declared that large haciendas should be broken up and the excess lands granted to peasants. These land reform measures were to be enforced throughout Mexico.

The Plan of Ayala was designed to end the revolution. However, it was never adopted. The revolution continued for nine more violent years. Land reform finally came, but never in the sweeping form that Zapata envisioned. Still, the Plan of Ayala was a dramatic attempt to end a war and give land to the landless. The attempt alone established Zapata as one of the greatest heroes in Mexican history.

Many poor farmers took up arms and fought in the revolution.

Chapter Three

A Deepening War

The Mexican Revolution became a fire that no one could control. In the countryside, generals fought other generals. The entire population was engulfed by war. Women and children followed male soldiers into battle. When a soldier fell, a woman picked up his rifle. When she was killed, the oldest child became a fighter. Men and women fought, even though they no longer understood why this terrible war raged in the land.

A character in *The Underdogs,* a novel written during the revolution, said, "You will ask me why I stay in the Revolution? The Revolution is a hurricane. The man who is swept up in it is no longer a man; he is a wretched dry leaf snatched away by the gale."

As the fighting dragged on, central leadership in Mexico vanished. General Huerta resigned as president in July 1914. During his 16-month term, Huerta had managed to steal more than 1 million pesos from the national budget. After Huerta, presidents came and left office in a confusing parade. Between 1913 and 1920, ten different presidents ruled Mexico. One president held office for only 46 minutes.

Individual leaders became more important than causes during the decade-long war. Soldiers identified themselves through their commanders rather than the principles

When General Victoriano Huerta resigned as president of Mexico he fled to Spain. Then, in 1915, he traveled to the United States and was arrested there on charges of promoting rebellion in Mexico. He died in prison on January 13, 1916.

for which they fought. The men and women who fought for Villa became the Villistas, and Zapata's followers were the Zapatistas.

In August 1914, Zapata and Villa traveled to Mexico City. There they were scheduled to meet two other rebel generals, Venustiano Carranza and Alvaro Obregón. The generals hoped to gather in the capital and discuss the nation's future. Mexico City residents bolted their doors, terrified over the meeting. The object of their fear was Zapata and his mostly Indian army. For hundreds of years, the whites and mixed-race people of Mexico lived in dread of an uprising by the country's Indian population. Now, they believed, the race war

Alvaro Obregón (right) lost his right arm during a battle in 1915.

No one really knows how many people were killed during the Mexican Revolution of 1910–1920. At least 1 million people died in the fighting or by starvation or disease brought about by the warfare. Some estimates say as many as 2 million Mexicans lost their lives in the conflict's 10-year span.

had come. Zapata and his dark-skinned Indians would destroy Mexico City and kill all its residents.

The Zapatistas entered Mexico City quietly and with dignity. They marched under the banner of the Virgin of Guadalupe, the Catholic symbol of Mexico. Groups of Zapatistas stopped and made the sign of the cross when they passed a church. They bought food at stores. When the stores closed, they knocked on doors and politely asked the residents for water and tortillas. By contrast, Villa's men stormed into the capital shooting guns in the air. The Villistas looted stores and assaulted men and women on the streets.

The conference among the four generals proved to be a dismal failure. Each military leader, except Zapata, wanted to control the government himself. No one could agree on how to stop the fighting and bring peace to the country. Zapata grew disgusted with the meeting and returned to his home in the south.

Pancho Villa (center) and Emiliano Zapata (to his right) were two of the four revolutionary leaders who met in Mexico City in 1914. Each man had his own band of loyal soldiers.

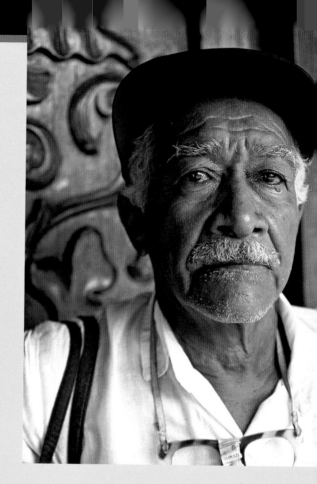

Beginning in the 1500s, many thousands of Spaniards and other Europeans streamed into Mexico. This mass migration gave the country three races—white Europeans (who were mostly from Spain), the mestizos (mixed-race people), and the native Indians. Under Spanish rule, the white Europeans owned most of the land and wealth. The mestizos were given meager privileges. The Indians were looked upon as a conquered race. Even after Mexico achieved independence in 1821, unequal treatment of the races remained a custom. In some communities, Indian people were forbidden even to sit on a park bench.

Today, the overwhelming majority of Mexicans are mestizos. An exact breakdown of the races is impossible to obtain because the government stopped using racial classification in the 1920 census. Discrimination against Indians ended as an official practice long ago.

The Zapata Legacy

Zapata (seated, center) had many supporters who would have been happy to see him become president of Mexico.

If Emiliano Zapata had become president of Mexico, his followers would have been overjoyed. But Zapata shunned all political offices. Instead, he built what amounted to a separate society in the state of Morelos. The society was based on the Plan of Ayala. All peasants owned the land they farmed. The people also ran a sugar mill and a primitive factory that refurbished old rifles. A Zapatista mint stamped out silver coins that were used as money in the state of Morelos.

Zapata (on horseback, fourth from left) and his brother (on horseback, third from left) ride with Zapatistas during the revolution.

As the revolution continued, the hacienda war grew in fury. Captured Zapatistas were hanged from trees by hacienda police. The police burned crops and houses belonging to Zapata's followers. Zapata used simple phrases to keep up the spirits of his fighters: "Men of the south, it is better to die on your feet than to live on your knees." Throughout the revolution, the Zapatista battle cry remained *Tierra y Libertad!*—Land and Liberty!

In March 1917, General Venustiano Carranza became president of Mexico. Zapata believed Carranza had betrayed the goals of the revolution. In a letter, Zapata told the president, "You took justice in your own hands and created a dictatorship which you gave the name 'Revolution.'"

A furious President Carranza sent an army to Morelos to capture and kill Zapata. But in the south, Zapata was nearly **invincible.** His followers knew every hill and mountain peak, every twist of the roads. All would lay down their lives to protect their leader. The Zapatistas attacked army camps at night, driving off horses and shooting soldiers. During the day, the rebel fighters became innocent farmworkers who claimed they had never heard of Zapata.

Venustiano Carranza became president of Mexico on May 1, 1917.

Unable to beat Zapata in battle, army leaders turned to trickery. A colonel named Guajardo sent word to one of Zapata's strongholds that he wished to switch sides. The colonel promised to bring many rifles and horses to the Zapatistas. On the morning of April 10, 1919, Zapata and 10 men rode to a hacienda where he was to meet Guajardo. A man inside the hacienda blew a bugle as if to salute the rebel leader. Then, on the last note of the bugle call, soldiers popped up on the tops of the hacienda walls. With a shattering roar, their rifles blazed. Zapata, struck by dozens of bullets, fell dead. Later, Zapata's bullet-ridden body was tied to a post in the central square of the town of Cuautla. The body remained there for several days so all could see that their valiant leader was dead.

Emiliano Zapata was murdered on April 10, 1919, at the age of 39.

The Mexican Revolution came to a close in 1920, largely because the people were too exhausted to fight anymore. Most of the goals of the revolution were never realized. Despite the noble battle cry—Land and Liberty!—many of Mexico's farmers remained poor and landless.

The memory of Emiliano Zapata remained burned into the people's minds. In fact, Mexicans of the south never accepted their leader's death. Zapata was the most unselfish leader of the revolution. He was also one of Mexico's finest horsemen. Years after his death, people claimed they still saw Emiliano Zapata on dim moonlit evenings. Always, he was mounted on a magnificent white horse. Always, he was riding alone.

A statue of Zapata on horseback honors his memory in Cuernavaca, Mexico.

Beginning in the 1990s, bands of gunmen began taking over land and entire towns in the southern state of Chiapas. The rebels claimed they wanted to bring land

reform and Indian rights to Chiapas. Government leaders denounced the rebels as communists and terrorists, but the movement captured the fancy of the Mexican public. The rebels called themselves the Zapatistas.

1876: General Porfirio Díaz becomes president of Mexico. Díaz stops a series of civil wars, but his policies favor rich landowners.

1879: Emiliano Zapata is born on August 8.

1894: Zapata's parents die, leaving him in charge of the family farm.

1909: Villagers from Anenecuilco who have lost their lands to a hacienda ask Zapata to appeal their case to the governor of Morelos. Zapata agrees, but his complaints are dismissed by the governor.

1910: Rebellions against the Mexican government begin under Pancho Villa in the north and Emiliano Zapata in the south.

1911: President Porfirio Díaz leaves office after governing Mexico for more than 30 years. Francisco Madero is elected president of Mexico. Emiliano Zapata issues the Plan of Ayala, which calls for land redistribution.

1912: Zapata builds a separate society in the state of Morelos. His followers take over hacienda land and farm it as if it were their own.

1913: Fighting between rival generals breaks out in Mexico City. General Victoriano Huerta has President Madero arrested. President Madero is kidnapped and later shot and killed. On Huerta's orders, rebel armies in the north wage war against Huerta.

1914: Huerta escapes from Mexico City and flees to Cuba. Mexico City is occupied by troops loyal to Generals Villa, Zapata, Carranza, and Obregón when the four men agree to meet to discuss future plans. Zapata's troops are well behaved, while Villa's soldiers loot stores and assault people. Zapata leaves Mexico City and returns to his home in Morelos.

1917: General Venustiano Carranza proclaims himself president of Mexico. Zapata claims Carranza has betrayed the revolution.

1916–1918: Zapata continues to implement the Plan of Ayala in southern Mexico. Carranza sends army units to the south to battle the Zapatistas.

1919: On April 10, Zapata is tricked into meeting a colonel who is under the command of Carranza. Before the meeting begins, Zapata is ambushed, shot, and killed by dozens of soldiers.

1920: President Carranza is killed while trying to gather an army. Alvaro Obregón becomes president and brings stability to the nation. The Mexican Revolution ends.

confiscated (CON-fuh-skate-ed) Something that is confiscated is taken illegally, or stolen. The hacienda land was originally confiscated from the peasant farmers.

demolish (di-MOL-ish) To demolish means to destroy or tear down. The landowner intended to demolish the houses.

dictator (DIK-tay-tur) A dictator is someone who takes over a country, often by force, and rules unjustly. President Díaz ruled Mexico as a dictator.

groomed (GROOMED) If an animal is groomed, it is brushed and cleaned. Zapata groomed his horses until their coats gleamed.

invincible (in-VIN-suh-buhl) Someone who is invincible cannot be defeated. Zapata was invincible in the south.

legend (LEJ-uhnd) Stories that are handed down over the years and may be based in fact, but are not completely true, are legends. The story about Zapata and his father is probably a legend.

militaristic (mil-ih-ta-RIS-tik) Something that is militaristic has to do with the military and the ideals of being prepared for war. The words to Mexico's national anthem are militaristic.

turmoil (TUR-moil) Turmoil is great confusion and unrest. Zapata lived during a time of turmoil in Mexico.

Books

Milord, Susan, and Michael P. Kline (illustrator). *Mexico: 40 Activities to Experience Mexico Past and Present.* Charlotte, Vt.: Williamson Publishing, 2003.

Stefoff, Rebecca. *Independence and Revolution in Mexico: 1810–1940.* New York: Facts on File, 1993.

Stein, R. Conrad. *Mexico.* New York: Childrens Press, 1998.

Stein, R. Conrad. *The Mexican Revolution 1910–1920.* New York: Macmillan, 1994.

Web Sites

Visit our Web page for lots of links about Emiliano Zapata:
http://www.childsworld.com/links.html

Note to parents, teachers, and librarians: We routinely check our Web links to make sure they're safe, active sites—so encourage your readers to check them out!

About the Author

R. Conrad Stein was born in Chicago, Illinois. At age 18, he enlisted in the U.S. Marines and served for three years. He later attended the University of Illinois and earned a degree in history. Mr. Stein is a full-time writer. Over the years, he has published more than 150 books, mostly history and geography titles. The author was especially pleased to write for A Proud Heritage because he lived in Mexico for seven years during the 1970s. The Stein family still spends most of the summer months in the town of San Miguel de Allende in central Mexico. The rest of the year, Mr. Stein lives in Chicago with his wife, children's book author Deborah Kent, and their daughter, Janna.